Increase Your Personality Power

TIM LaHAYE

POCKET GUIDES
Tyndale House Publishers, Inc.
Wheaton, Illinois

Adapted from *Your Temperament: Discover Its Potential* by Tim LaHaye, copyright 1984 by Tim LaHaye.

First printing, April 1986
Library of Congress Catalog Card Number 85-52233
ISBN 0-8423-1604-3
Copyright 1986 by Tim LaHaye
All rights reserved
Printed in the United States of America

CONTENTS

Why You Act
the Way You Do

Everyone is interested in human behavior. That is why over 80 percent of our nation's thirteen million college students voluntarily take psychology classes; they are fascinated by what makes people tick. And most of all, they are interested in why they think, feel, respond, explode, and act the way they do.

Nothing answers those questions better than the theory of the four temperaments. It explains differences in people—their tastes, their creative capabilities, their strengths and weaknesses. It explains why some people conflict with others and why others are attracted to each other.

TEMPERAMENT—
YOU'RE BORN WITH IT

Humanly speaking, nothing has a more profound influence on your behavior than your inherited temperament. The combination of your parents' genes and chromosomes at conception, which determined your basic temperament nine months before you drew your first breath, is largely responsible for your actions, reactions, emotional responses, and, to one degree or another, almost everything you do.

Most people are completely unaware of this extremely powerful influence on their behavior. Consequently, instead of cooperating with it and using it, they conflict with this inner power and often try to make something of themselves that they were never intended to be. This not only limits them personally, but affects their immediate family and often spoils other interpersonal relationships. It is one of the reasons so many people say, "I don't like myself" or, "I can't find myself." When a person discovers his basic temperament and then his specific personality type, he can usually figure out rather easily what vocational opportunities he is best suited for, how to get along with other people, what natural weaknesses to watch for, what kind of spouse he should marry, and how he can improve the effectiveness of his life.

WHAT IS TEMPERAMENT?

Temperament is the combination of inborn traits that subconsciously affect our behavior. These traits are passed on by the genes. Some psychologists suggest that we get more genes from our grandparents than our parents. That could account for the greater resemblance of some children to their grandparents than to their parents. The alignment of temperament traits is just as unpredictable as the color of eyes and hair, or size of body.

It is a person's temperament that makes him outgoing and extroverted or shy and introverted. Doubtless you know both kinds of people who were born to the same parents. Similarly, it is temperament that makes some people art and music enthusiasts while others are sports- or industry-minded. In fact, I have met outstanding musicians whose siblings were tone-deaf.

Temperament is not the only influence upon our behavior, of course. Early home life, training, education, and motivation also exercise powerful influences on our actions throughout life.

Temperament, is, however, the first thing that affects us because, like body structure, color of eyes, and other physical characteristics, it escorts us through life. An extrovert is an extrovert. He may tone down the expression of his extroversion, but he will always be an extrovert. Similarly, although an introvert may be able to come out of his shell and act more aggressively, he will never be transformed into an extrovert. Temperament sets broad guidelines on everyone's behavior—patterns that will influence a person as long as he lives. On one side are his strengths, on the other his weaknesses. The primary advantage to learning about the four basic temperaments is to discover how to overcome your weaknesses and take advantage of your strengths.

MEET THE FOUR TEMPERAMENTS

The heart of the temperament theory, as first conceived by Hippocrates more than twenty-four hundred years ago, divides people into four basic categories: sanguine, choleric, melancholy, and phlegmatic. Each temperament type has both strengths and weaknesses that form a distinct part of his makeup throughout life. Once a person diagnoses his own basic temperament, he is better equipped to ascertain what vocational opportunities he is best suited for and what natural weaknesses he must work on to keep from short-circuiting his potential and creativity. The temperament chart on page 15 summarizes these strengths and weaknesses.

The following brief descriptions of four basic temperaments will introduce you to these four different types of people. No doubt you will identify several of your friends in one or another of these classifications, and if you look carefully, you may even discover one that reminds you of yourself.

MEET
SPARKY
SANGUINE

Sparky Sanguine is a warm, buoyant, lively, and "enjoying" person. Receptive by nature, external impressions easily find their way to his heart, where they cause an outburst of response. Feelings rather than reflective thoughts predominate to form his decisions.

Sparky is so outgoing he is usually considered a superextrovert. He has an unusual capacity for enjoying himself and usually passes on his fun-loving spirit. The moment he enters a room he tends to lift the spirits of everyone present by his exuberant conversation. He is a fascinating storyteller and his warm, emotional nature almost helps you relive the experience as he tells it.

Mr. Sanguine never lacks for friends. He can genuinely feel the joys and sorrows of the person he meets and has the capacity to make him feel important, as though he were a very special friend—and he is, as long as Mr. Sanguine is looking at him. Then he fixes his eyes with equal intensity on the next person he meets.

My sanguine minister friend Ken Poure says, "A sanguine always enters a room mouth first." His noisy, blustering, friendly ways make him appear more confident than he really is, but his energy and lovable disposition get him by the rough spots of life. People have a way of excusing his weaknesses by saying, "That's just the way he is."

MEET
ROCKY
CHOLERIC

Rocky Choleric is hot, quick, active, practical, strong-willed, self-sufficient, and very independent. He tends to be decisive and opinionated, finding it easy to make decisions both for himself and other people. Like Sparky Sanguine, Rocky Choleric is an extrovert, but is not nearly so intense.

Mr. Choleric thrives on activity. He does not need to be stimulated by his environment, but rather stimulates his environment with his endless ideas, plans, goals, and ambitions. He does not engage in aimless activity, for he has a practical, keen mind, capable of making sound, instant decisions or planning worthwhile projects. He does not vacillate under the pressure of what others think, but takes a definite stand on issues and can often be found crusading against some social injustice or subversive situation.

Mr. Choleric's emotional nature is the least developed part of his temperament. He does not sympathize easily with others, nor does he naturally show or express compassion. He is often embarrassed or disgusted by the tears of others and is usually insensitive to their needs. He reflects little appreciation for music and the fine arts, unless his secondary temperament traits are those of the melancholy. He invariably seeks utilitarian and productive values in life.

Not given to analysis, but rather to quick, almost intuitive appraisal, the choleric tends to look at the goal for which he is working without recognizing the potential pitfalls and obstacles in the path. Once he has started toward his goal, he may run roughshod over individuals who stand in his way. He tends to be domineering and bossy and does not hesitate to use people to accomplish his ends. He is often considered an opportunist.

MEET
MARTIN
MELANCHOLY

Martin Melancholy is the richest of all the temperaments. He is an analytical, self-sacrificing, gifted, perfectionist type with a very sensitive emotional nature. No one gets more enjoyment from the fine arts than the melancholy. By nature, he is prone to be an introvert; but since his feelings predominate, he is given to a variety of moods.

Martin is a very faithful friend, but unlike the sanguine, he does not make friends easily. He seldom pushes himself forward to meet people, but rather lets them come to him. He is perhaps the most dependable of all the temperaments, for his perfectionist and conscientious tendencies do not permit him to be a shirker or let others down when they are counting on him. His reticence to put himself forward is often taken as an indication that he doesn't enjoy people. Like the rest of us, he not only likes others but has a strong desire to be loved by them. However, he finds it difficult to express his true feelings.

His exceptional analytical ability causes him to diagnose accurately the obstacles and dangers of any project he has a part in planning. This is in sharp contrast to the choleric. Such a characteristic often finds the melancholy reticent to initiate some new project or in conflict with those who wish to do so. Occasionally, in a mood of emotional ecstasy or inspiration, he may produce some great work of art or genius.

Martin Melancholy usually finds his greatest meaning in life through personal sacrifice. He seems desirous of making himself suffer, and he will often choose a difficult life vocation. But once it is chosen, he is prone to be very thorough and persistent in his pursuit of it and more than likely will accomplish great good if his natural tendency to gripe throughout the sacrificial process doesn't get him so depressed that he gives up on it altogether.

MEET
PHILIP
PHELGMATIC

Philip Phlegmatic is the calm, easygoing, never-get-upset individual with such a high boiling point that he almost never becomes angry. He is the easiest type of person to get along with and is by nature the most likable of all the temperaments.

Philip Phlegmatic derives his name from what Hippocrates thought was the body fluid that produced that "calm, cool, slow, well-balanced temperament." Life for him is a happy, unexcited, pleasant experience in which he avoids as much involvement as possible. He is so calm and unruffled that he never seems agitated, no matter what circumstances surround him. He is the one temperament type that is consistent every time you see him.

Beneath his cool, reticent, almost timid personality, Mr. Phlegmatic has a very capable combination of abilities. He feels more emotion than appears on the surface and appreciates the fine arts and the beautiful things of life. Usually he avoids violence.

The phlegmatic does not lack for friends because he enjoys people and has a natural, dry sense of humor. He is the type of individual who can have a crowd of people "in stitches," yet never cracks a smile. Possessing the unique capability for seeing something humorous in others and the things they do, he maintains a positive approach to life. He has a good, retentive mind.

Phil Phlegmatic tends to be a spectator in life and tries not to get very involved with the activities of others. In fact, it is usually with great reluctance that he is ever motivated to any form of activity beyond his daily routine. This does not mean, however, that he cannot appreciate the need for action and the predicaments of others.

Usually kindhearted and sympathetic, Phil Phlegmatic seldom conveys his true feelings. When once aroused to action, however, his capable and efficient qualities become apparent. He will not volunteer to leadership on his own, but when it is forced upon him, he proves to be a very capable leader. He has a conciliating effect on others and is a natural peacemaker.

PEOPLE ARE DIFFERENT
Now that you have met the four temperaments, you no doubt realize why "people are individuals." Not only are there four distinct types of temperaments that produce these

FOUR BASIC TEMPERAMENTS

SANGUINE

Strengths	Weaknesses
outgoing	undisciplined
responsive	emotionally
warm &	unstable
friendly	unproductive
talkative	egocentric
enthusiastic	exaggerates
compassionate	

CHOLERIC

Strengths	Weaknesses
strong-willed	cold &
independent	unemotional
visionary	self-sufficient
practical	impetuous
productive	domineering
decisive	unforgiving
leader	sarcastic
	angry
	cruel

MELANCHOLY

Strengths	Weaknesses
gifted	moody
analytical	self-centered
aesthetic	persecution-
self-sacrificing	prone
industrious	revengeful
self-disciplined	touchy
	theoretical
	unsociable
	critical
	negative

PHLEGMATIC

Strengths	Weaknesses
calm, quiet	unmotivated
easy-going	procrastinator
dependable	selfish
objective	stingy
diplomatic	self-protective
efficient,	indecisive
organized	fearful
practical	worrier
humorous	

differences, but the combinations, mixtures, and degrees of temperament multiply the possible differences in personality. In spite of that, however, most people reveal a pattern of behavior that indicates they lean toward one predominant type.

Recently I had an experience that graphically portrayed the difference of temperament. It was necessary for me to find a Thermofax machine while speaking at a summer high school camp. In the small town nearby, the only one available was in the education center. When I arrived by appointment, I found nine people hard at work. The calm, orderly, and efficient surroundings made me realize that I was in the presence of individuals of predominantly melancholy or phlegmatic temperament.

This was later confirmed as the superintendent carefully computed my bill and refused my money because it was "against the rules." Instead he took me to the meticulous treasurer, who took us to the bookkeeper, who in turn relayed us to the cashier, who finally arranged for me to give my $1.44 to the switchboard operator, who kept the petty cash, lest some of their bookkeeping records would have to be altered. The clincher was the petty cash box, which clearly revealed the touch of a perfectionist. The change had been carefully stacked in neat piles of quarters, dimes, and nickels.

As I surveyed the placid environment and noted their calm but definite concern for this minor problem, my mind flitted hilariously to the scene of the sales office where they had sold the overhead projector. There the sales staff, chief executive, and all the employees were predominantly of the extrovertish choleric or sanguine temperaments. The place was a disorganized mess! Papers were strewn everywhere, telephones and desks were unattended, the office was a hubbub of noisy activity. Finally, above the din of voices, I heard the sales manager say to the staff, with a look of desperation, "One of these days we are going to get organized around here!"

These two scenes show the natural contrast of the inherited traits that produce human temperament. They also point out the fact that all four of the basic temperaments we have described are needed for variety and purposefulness. *No single personality type can be said to be better than another.* Each one contains strengths and richness, and yet each one is fraught with its own weaknesses and dangers. How to improve your weaknesses is the purpose of this book.

Do's and Don'ts of the Temperament Theory

1. *Do not use it to embarrass your friends.* No one likes to be stripped psychologically bare.
2. *Do not use it to excuse your weaknesses.* If you condone your weaknesses by saying, "It's because of my temperament," you won't help yourself.
3. *Do not use it to categorize people.* First, snap decisions can be wrong. Second, it's sometimes easy to get caught up in the theory and analysis of temperament and in the process lose sight of the person and his or her real needs.
4. *Do use it to accept yourself.* This theory helps you to come to grips with who you really are.
5. *Do use it to improve yourself.* Once you have examined your weaknesses, call upon God for his resources to help you better yourself and your behavior.
6. *Do use it to understand and accept others.* When you understand why they do what they do, it is easier to accept and love them.

CHAPTER 2

Twelve Personality Types

The chief objection to the theory of the four temperaments as advocated by the ancients is that it was overly simplistic in assuming every person could be characterized by only one of the four temperaments. In an attempt to make the temperament theory more practical and true to life, we shall briefly examine twelve possible personality types. In all probability, you will find yourself here.

A VARIETY OF BLENDS

Essentially, each person is capable of possessing twenty strengths and twenty weaknesses to one degree or another (ten for the predominant temperament and ten for the secondary temperament). Some of them, as we shall see, cancel each other out, some reinforce each other, and some accentuate and compound others, accounting for the varieties of behavior, prejudices, and natural skills of people with the same predominant temperament but with different secondary temperaments. This will become clearer as you study the following twelve personality types.

THE SANCHLOR

The strongest extrovert of all the personality types will be the SanChlor, for the two temperaments that make up his nature are both extroverted. The happy charisma of the sanguine makes him a people-oriented, enthusiastic, salesman type; but the choleric side of his nature will provide him the necessary resolution and character traits that will fashion a somewhat more organized and productive individual than if he were pure sanguine. Almost any people-oriented field is open to him, but to sustain his interest it must offer variety, activity, and excitement.

The potential weaknesses of a SanChlor are usually apparent to everyone because he is such an external person. He customarily talks too much, thus exposing himself and his weaknesses for all to see. He is highly opinionated. Consequently, he expresses himself loudly even before he knows all the facts. To be honest, no one has more mouth trouble! If he is the life of the party, he is lovable; but if he feels threatened or insecure, he can become obnoxious. His leading emotional problem will be anger, which can catapult him into action at the slightest provocation. Since he combines the easy forgetfulness of the sanguine and the stubborn casuistry of the choleric, he may not have a very active conscience.

THE SANMEL

SanMels are highly emotional people who fluctuate drastically. They can laugh hysterically one minute and burst into tears the next. It is almost impossible for them to hear a sad tale, observe a tragic plight of another person, or listen to melancholic music without weeping profusely. They genuinely feel the griefs of others. Almost any field is open to them, especially public speaking, acting, music, and the fine arts.

SanMels reflect an uninhibited perfectionism that often alienates them from others because they verbalize their criticisms. They are usually people-oriented individuals who have sufficient substance to make a contribution to other lives—if their ego and arrogance don't make them so obnoxious that others become hostile to them.

One of the crucial weaknesses of this type

prevails in SanMel's thought-life. Both sanguines and melancholies are dreamers, and thus if the melancholy part of his nature suggests a negative train of thought, it can nullify a SanMel's potential. It is easy for him to get down on himself. In addition, this person, more than most others, will have both an anger problem and a tendency toward fear. Both temperaments in his makeup suffer with an insecurity problem; not uncommonly, he is fearful to utilize his potential. Being admired by others is so important to him that it will drive him to a consistent level of performance.

THE
SANPHLEG

The easiest person to like is a SanPhleg. The overpowering and obnoxious tendencies of a sanguine are offset by the gracious, easygoing phlegmatic. SanPhlegs are extremely happy people whose carefree spirit and good humor make them lighthearted entertainers sought after by others. Helping people is their regular business, along with sales of various kinds. They are the least extroverted of any of the sanguines and are often regulated by their environment and circumstances rather than being self-motivated. SanPhlegs are naturally pro-family and preserve the love of their children—and everyone else for that matter. They would not purposely hurt anyone.

The SanPhleg's greatest weaknesses are lack of motivation and discipline. He would rather socialize than work, and he tends to take life too casually. As an executive remarked about one, "He is the nicest guy I ever fired." He rarely gets upset over anything and tends to find the bright side of everything. He usually has an endless repertoire of jokes and delights in making others laugh, often when the occasion calls for seriousness.

THE CHLORSAN

The second-strongest extrovert among the personality types—the ChlorSan—will be the reverse of the first. This man's life is given over completely to activity. Most of his efforts are productive and purposeful, but watch his recreation—it is so activity-prone that it borders on being violent. He is a natural promoter and salesman, with enough charisma to get along well with others. Certainly the best motivator of people and one who thrives on a challenge, he is almost fearless and exhibits boundless energy. His wife will often comment, "He has only two speeds: wide open and stop."

Mr. ChlorSan is the courtroom attorney who can charm the coldest-hearted judge and jury, the fund-raiser who can get people to contribute what they intended to save, the man who never goes anywhere unnoticed, the preacher who combines both practical Bible teaching and church administration, and the politician who talks his state into changing its constitution so he can represent them one more time. A convincing debater, what he lacks in facts or arguments he makes up in bluff or bravado.

As a teacher, he is an excellent communicator, particularly in the social sciences; rarely is he drawn to math, science, or the abstract. Whatever his professional occupation, his brain is always in motion.

The weaknesses of this man, the chief of which is hostility, are as broad as his talents. He combines the quick, explosive anger of the sanguine (without the forgiveness) and the long-burning resentment of the choleric. He is the one personality type who not only gets ulcers himself, but gives them to others. Impatient with those who do not share his motivation and energy, he prides himself on being brutally frank (some call it sarcastically frank).

It is difficult for him to concentrate on one thing very long, which is why he often enlists others to finish what he has started. He is opinionated, prejudiced, impetuous, and inclined doggedly to finish a project he probably should not have started in the first place. Most ChlorSans get so engrossed in their work that they neglect wife and family, even lashing out at them if they complain. Once he comprehends the importance of giving love and approval to his family, however, he can transform his entire household.

THE CHLORMEL

The choleric/melancholy is an extremely industrious and capable person. The optimism and practicality of the choleric overcome the tendency toward moodiness of the melancholy, making the ChlorMel both goal-oriented and detailed. Such a person usually does well in school, possesses a quick, analytical mind, yet is decisive. He develops into a thorough leader, the kind whom one can always count on to do an extraordinary job. Never take him on in a debate unless you are assured of your facts, for he will make mincemeat of you, combining verbal aggressiveness and attendance to detail.

This person is extremely competitive and forceful in all that he does. He is a dogged researcher and is usually successful, no matter what kind of business he pursues. This personality type probably makes the best natural leader. General George S. Patton, the great commander of the U.S. Third Army in World War II who drove the German forces back to Berlin, was probably a ChlorMel.

Equally as great as his strengths are his weaknesses. He is apt to be autocratic, a dictator type who inspires admiration and hate simultaneously. He is usually a quick-witted talker whose sarcasm can devastate others. He is a natural-born crusader whose work habits are irregular and long.

A ChlorMel harbors considerable hostility and resentment, and unless he enjoys a good love relationship with his parents, he will find interpersonal relationships difficult, particularly with his family. No man is more apt to be an overly strict disciplinarian than the ChlorMel father. He combines the hard-to-please tendency of the choleric and the perfectionism of the melancholy.

THE CHLORPHLEG

The most subdued of all the extrovert temperaments is the ChlorPhleg, a happy blend of the quick, active, and hot with the calm, cool, and unexcited. He is not as apt to rush into things as quickly as the preceding extroverts because he is more deliberate and subdued. He is extremely capable in the long run, although he does not particularly impress you that way at first. He is a very organized person who combines planning and hard work.

People usually enjoy working with and for him because he knows where he is going and has charted his course, yet is not unduly severe with people. He has the ability to help others make the best use of their skills and rarely offends people or makes them feel used.

The ChlorPhleg's slogan on organization states: "Anything that needs to be done can be done better if it's organized." These people are usually good spouses and parents as well as excellent administrators in almost any field.

In spite of his obvious capabilities, the

ChlorPhleg is not without a notable set of weaknesses. Although not as addicted to the quick anger of some temperaments, he is known to harbor resentment and bitterness. Some of the cutting edge of the choleric's sarcasm is here offset by the gracious spirit of the phlegmatic; so instead of uttering cutting and cruel remarks, his barbs are more apt to emerge as cleverly disguised humor. One is never quite sure whether he is kidding or ridiculing, depending on his mood.

No one can be more bullheadedly stubborn than a ChlorPhleg, and it is very difficult for him to change his mind once it is committed. Repentance or the acknowledgment of a mistake is not at all easy for him. Consequently, he will be more apt to make it up to those he has wronged without really facing his mistake. The worrisome traits of the phlegmatic side of his nature may so curtail his adventurous tendencies that he never quite measures up to his capabilities.

Now we turn to the predominantly introverted personality types. Each will look somewhat similar to one we have already examined, except that the two temperaments making up their nature will be reversed in intensity. Such variation accounts for the exciting individuality in human beings.

THE MELSAN

Mr. MelSan is usually a very gifted person, fully capable of being a musician who can steal the heart of an audience. As an artist, he not only draws or paints beautifully but can sell his own work—if he's in the right mood. It is not uncommon to encounter him in the field of education, for he makes a good scholar and probably the best of all classroom teachers, particularly on the high school and college level. The melancholy in him will ferret out little-known facts and be exacting in the use of events and detail, while the sanguine will enable him to communicate well with students.

Mr. MelSan shows an interesting combination of mood swings. Be sure of this: he is an emotional creature! When circumstances are pleasing to him, he can reflect a fantastically happy mood. But if things work out badly or he is rejected, insulted, or injured, he drops into such a mood that his lesser sanguine nature drowns in the resultant sea of self-pity. He is easily moved to tears, feels everything deeply, but can be unreasonably critical and hard on others. He tends to be rigid and usually will not cooperate unless things go his way, which is often idealistic and impractical. He is often a fearful, insecure man with a poor self-image which limits him unnecessarily.

THE MELCHLOR

The mood swings of the melancholy are usually stabilized by the choleric's self-will and determination. There is almost nothing vocationally this man cannot do—and do well. He is both a perfectionist and a driver. He possesses strong leadership capabilities. Almost any craft, construction, or educational level is open to him. Unlike the MelSan, he may found his own institution or business and run it capably—not with noise and color but with efficiency. Many a great orchestra leader and choral conductor is a MelChlor.

The natural weaknesses of MelChlors reveal themselves in the mind, emotions, and mouth. They are extremely difficult people to please, rarely satisfying even themselves. Once they start thinking negatively about something or someone (including themselves), they can be intolerable to live with. Their moods follow their thought processes.

Although they do not retain a depressed mood as long as the other blends of the melancholy, they can lapse into it more quickly. The two basic temperaments haunted by self-persecution, hostility, and criticism are the melancholy and the choleric. It is not uncommon for him to get angry at God as well as his fellowman, and if such thoughts persist long enough he may become manic-depressive. In extreme cases, he can become sadistic. When confronted with his vile thinking pattern and angry, bitter spirit, he can be expected to explode.

His penchant for detailed analysis and perfection tends to make him a nitpicker who drives others up the wall. Unless he can maintain a positive frame of mind, he is not enjoyable company for long periods of time. No one is more painfully aware of this than his wife and children. He not only "emotes" disapproval, but feels compelled to castigate them verbally for their failures and to correct their mistakes—in public as well as in private.

THE MELPHLEG

Some of the greatest scholars the world has ever known have been MelPhlegs. They are not nearly as prone to hostility as the two previous melancholies and usually get along well with others. These gifted introverts combine the analytical perfectionism of the melancholy with the organized efficiency of the phlegmatic. They are usually good-natured humanitarians who prefer a quiet, solitary environment for study and research to the endless rounds of activities sought by the more extroverted types.

MelPhlegs are usually excellent spellers and good mathematicians. These gifted people have greatly benefited humanity. Most of the world's significant inventions and medical discoveries have been made by Mel-Phlegs.

Despite his abilities, the MelPhleg, like the rest of us, has his own weaknesses. He can easily become discouraged and develop a very negative thinking pattern. But once he learns to rejoice, his entire outlook on life can be transformed. Ordinarily a quiet person, he is capable of inner angers and hostility caused by his tendency to be vengeful.

MelPhlegs are unusually vulnerable to fear, anxiety, and a negative self-image. It has always amazed me that the people with the greatest talents and capabilities are often victimized by genuine feelings of poor self-worth. Their strong tendency to be conscientious allows them to let others pressure them into making commitments that drain their energy and creativity.

These people are often loved and admired by their family because their personal self-discipline and dedication are exemplary in the home. But humanitarian concerns can cause them to neglect their family. Unless they learn to pace themselves and enjoy diversions that help them relax, they often become early mortality statistics.

THE PHLEGSAN

The easiest of the twelve personality types to get along with over a protracted period of time is the PhlegSan. He is congenial, happy, cooperative, thoughtful, people-oriented, diplomatic, dependable, fun-loving, and humorous. A favorite with children and adults, he never displays an abrasive side. He is usually a good family man who enjoys a quiet life and loves his wife and children. Ordinarily he attends a church where the pastor is a good motivator; there he probably takes an active role.

The weaknesses of a PhlegSan are as gentle as his personality—unless you have to live with him all the time. Since he inherited the lack of motivation of a phlegmatic and the lack of discipline of a sanguine, it is not uncommon for the PhlegSan to fall far short of his true capabilities. He often quits school, passes up good opportunities, and avoids anything that involves "too much effort."

Fear is another problem that accentuates his unrealistic feelings of insecurity. With more faith, he could grow beyond his timidity and self-defeating anxieties. However, he prefers to build a self-protective shell around himself and selfishly avoids the kind of involvement or commitment to activity that he needs and that would be a rich blessing to his partner and children.

THE PHLEGCHLOR

The most active of all phlegmatics is the PhlegChlor. But it must be remembered that since he is predominantly a phlegmatic, he will never be a ball of fire. Like his brother phlegmatics, he is easy to get along with and may become an excellent group leader.

The phlegmatic has the potential to become a good counselor, for he is an excellent listener, does not interrupt the client with stories about himself, and is genuinely interested in other people. Although the PhlegChlor rarely offers his services to others, when they come to his organized office where he exercises control, he is a first-rate professional. His advice will be practical and helpful. His gentle spirit never makes people feel threatened.

He always does the right thing, but rarely goes beyond the norm. If his wife can make the adjustment to his passive life-style and reluctance to take the lead in the home, particularly in the discipline of their children, they can enjoy a happy marriage.

The weaknesses of the PhlegChlor are not readily apparent but gradually come to the surface, especially in the home. In addition to the lack of motivation and the fear problems of other phlegmatics, he can be determinedly stubborn and unyielding. He doesn't blow up at others, but simply refuses to give in or cooperate. He is not a fighter by nature, but often lets his inner anger and stubbornness reflect itself in silence.

The PhlegChlor often retreats to his "workshop" alone or nightly immerses his mind in TV. The older he gets, the more he selfishly indulges his sedentary tendency and becomes increasingly passive. Although he will probably live a long and peaceful life, if he indulges these passive feelings it is a boring life—not only for him, but also for his family. He needs to give himself to the concerns and needs of his family.

THE PHLEGMEL

Of all the personality types the PhlegMel is the most gracious, gentle, and quiet. He is rarely angry or hostile and almost never says anything for which he must apologize (mainly because he rarely says much). He never embarrasses himself or others, always does the proper thing, dresses simply, is dependable and exact. He tends to have the spiritual gifts of mercy and help, and he is neat and organized in his working habits.

Like any phlegmatic, he is handy around the house and as energy permits will keep his home in good repair. If he has a spouse who recognizes his tendencies toward passivity, they will have a good family life and marriage. He may neglect the discipline necessary to help prepare his children for a productive, self-disciplined life and so "provoke his children to wrath" just as much as the angry tyrant whose unreasonable discipline makes them bitter.

The other weaknesses of this man revolve around fear, selfishness, negativism, criticism, and lack of self-image. Once a PhlegMel realizes that only his fears and negative feelings about himself keep him from succeeding, he is able to come out of his shell and become an effective person, marriage partner, and parent. Most PhlegMels are so afraid of overextending themselves or getting overly involved that they automatically refuse almost any kind of affiliation.

Personally I have never seen a PhlegMel overinvolved in anything—except in keeping from getting overinvolved. He must recognize that since he is not internally motivated, he definitely needs to accept more responsibility than he thinks he can fulfill, for that external stimulation will motivate him to greater achievement. All phlegmatics work well under outside pressure.

CHAPTER 3

Which Personality Type Are You?

One day an industrial psychologist from the Midwest was visiting San Diego. He invited me to lunch with his family and, since my wife was out of town speaking at a women's conference, I accepted.

We had barely returned from the buffet with our food when he said, "I have used your temperament theory in vocational counseling for ten years and find it the most helpful tool for vocational guidance I have ever seen."

Here was a man with a Ph.D. in psychology who served as a consultant to the major aircraft companies of the nation and who recognized that the four-temperament theory is the best single theory of human behavior yet devised. It isn't perfect, and it is not accepted universally, but it is an excellent aid to many things, particularly vocational guidance.

My psychologist friend then asked, "Have you developed a personality test? If so, I'd like to see it." At that time I had to respond, "Not yet. I'm working on one, but I'm not satisfied with it." That was seven years ago and five tests back. I am very satisfied with the one I use now—The LaHaye Temperament Analysis—which is extremely thorough.* But I also developed some simple personality tests you can give yourself or have some of your friends give you.

TEMPERAMENT TEST

Three charts are given for your personal use. *Chart 1* is to determine how you see yourself. *Charts 2 and 3* are to give your best friends to do on you. Then you can compare the average of your friends' charts with your own temperament blob chart to see if your perception of you is similar to the way your friends see you. If not, then you need to ask yourself if you really are objective about yourself or if you project a face to others so they see you as you want them to, rather than as you really are.

Chart 1: Your Personal Profile
Instructions:

1. Relax, get in a quiet place, and read the entire chart on pages 42 and 43 before making any markings.

2. After each word on the circle, place a dot on the numbered line that best describes you, 5 being the most like you and 1 being the least like you. Try to be objective and do not use more than twenty-five minutes.

*The LaHaye Temperament Analysis consists of four tests in one to allow for comparison. Each analysis is personally prepared and presented in a thirteen- to seventeen-page summary. Currently it is not available in bookstores, but can be purchased from Family Life Seminars, P.O. Box 16000, San Diego, CA 92116.

Charts 2 and 3: Your Friends Analyze You

The charts on pages 44-47 are for two of your best friends to use in analyzing you. Ask each friend to fill out one chart with your characteristics, strengths, and weaknesses. Have each friend read the following instructions:

1. Read all the adjectives below before making a mark.

2. After each word on the chart, place a dot on the numbered line that best describes your friend—1 being least like him and 5 being most like him.

3. Try to be objective, indicating what he is like most of the time.

Scoring Your Temperament Chart

Instructions:

1. Average only the 3, 4, and 5 dots listed in charts 2 and 3 (omit the 1s and 2s—they are of such low intensity that they do not influence this test).

2. Place the average totals from Charts 2 and 3 on Chart 1, using a different color pen.

3. Connect the dots from Charts 2 and 3 by drawing curved lines paralleling the basic circles from dot to dot except when nothing appears in a temperament quadrant. Follow the outer edge of the quadrant to the center, then return to the next dot.

4. Connect your dots as in Step 3.

Assessing the Results

Chart 1 now contains two blobs of different colors. Ideally the blobs will be identical. In most cases there will be some variation. However, your primary temperament should stand out as the larger blob. Hopefully, both large blobs will be in the same temperament zone. If they are not, something for you to think about is, "Do my friends see me as I see myself, or is there a great difference?" If two of your friends' scores were quite similar to your own, then disregard the third chart altogether. Some people read too much into a simple test like this. Consequently, their excessive scores will completely alter the averages of your other friends.

On the other hand, if your score and that of your friends is in marked contrast, then it may mean you are trying to make yourself something God never intended you to be. You need to realistically face yourself as you really are.

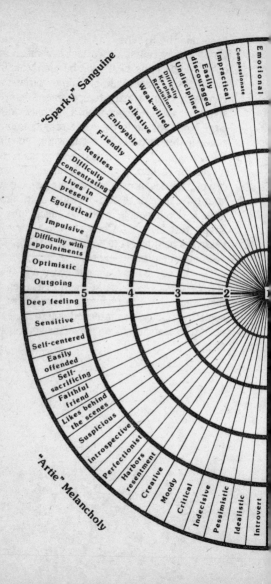

"Sparky" Sanguine

Emotional
Compassionate
Impractical
Easily discouraged
Undisciplined
Difficulty Keeping Resolutions
Weak-willed
Talkative
Enjoyable
Friendly
Restless
Difficulty concentrating
Lives in present
Egotistical
Impulsive
Difficulty with appointments
Optimistic
Outgoing

5 4 3 2

Deep feeling
Sensitive
Self-centered
Easily offended
Self-sacrificing
Faithful friend
Likes behind the scenes
Suspicious
Introspective
Perfectionist
Harbors resentment
Creative
Moody
Critical
Indecisive
Pessimistic
Idealistic
Introvert

"Artie" Melancholy

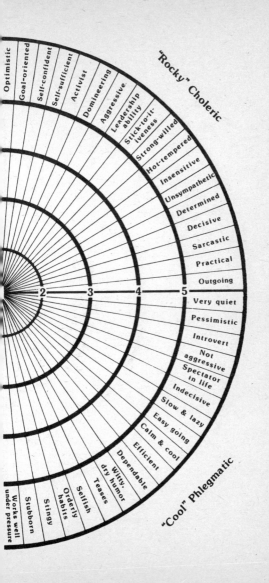

"Rocky" Choleric

Optimistic
Goal-oriented
Self-confident
Self-sufficient
Activist
Domineering
Aggressive
Leadership ability
Stick-to-it-iveness
Strong-willed
Hot-tempered
Insensitive
Unsympathetic
Determined
Decisive
Sarcastic
Practical
Outgoing

2   3   4   5

Very quiet
Pessimistic
Introvert
Not aggressive
Spectator in life
Indecisive
Slow & lazy
Easy going
Calm & cool
Efficient
Dependable
Witty, dry humor
Teases
Selfish
Orderly habits
Stingy
Stubborn
Works well under pressure

"Cool" Phlegmatic

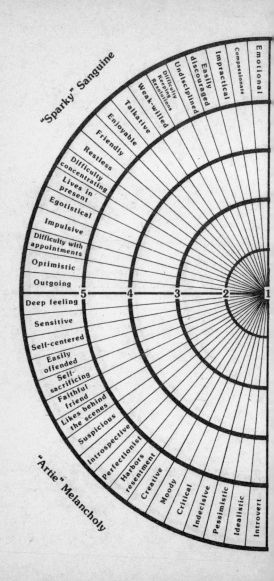

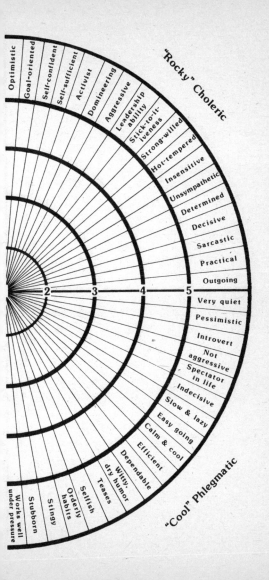

"Rocky" Choretic

Optimistic
Goal-oriented
Self-confident
Self-sufficient
Activist
Domineering
Aggressive
Leadership ability
Stick-to-it-iveness
Strong-willed
Hot-tempered
Insensitive
Unsympathetic
Determined
Decisive
Sarcastic
Practical
Outgoing

2   3   4   5

Very quiet
Pessimistic
Introvert
Not aggressive
Spectator in life
Indecisive
Slow & lazy
Easy going
Calm & cool
Efficient
Dependable
Witty, dry humor.
Teases
Selfish
Orderly habits
Stingy
Stubborn
Works well under pressure

"Cool" Phlegmatic

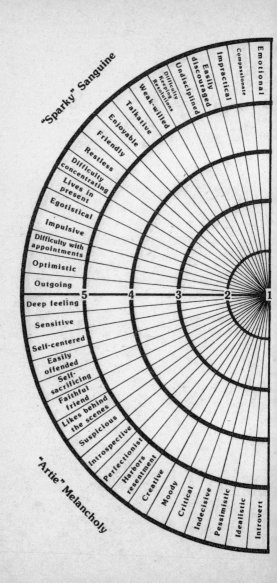

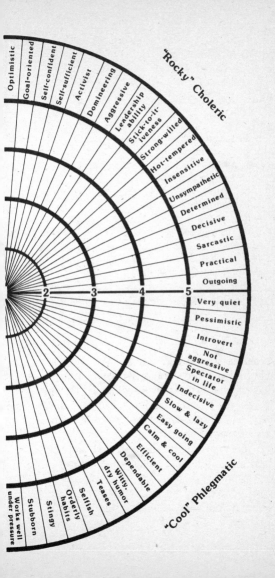

'Rocky' Choleric

Optimistic
Goal-oriented
Self-confident
Self-sufficient
Activist
Domineering
Aggressive
Leadership ability
Stick-to-it-iveness
Strong-willed
Hot-tempered
Insensitive
Unsympathetic
Determined
Decisive
Sarcastic
Practical
Outgoing

2 — 3 — 4 — 5

Very quiet
Pessimistic
Introvert
Not aggressive
Spectator in life
Indecisive
Slow & lazy
Easy going
Calm & cool
Efficient
Dependable
Witty, dry humor
Teases
Selfish
Orderly habits
Stingy
Stubborn
Works well under pressure

'Cool' Phlegmatic

SELF-QUIZ

If you are not satisfied with the accuracy of the above temperament blob, here are some questions to ask yourself.

	Yes	No
1. Are you an extrovert?	____	____
2. Are you a spontaneous quick-talker?	____	____
3. Do you have to apologize frequently?	____	____
4. Do you have high emotional responses?	____	____
5. Are you quiet and slow of speech?	____	____
6. Are you a good speller?	____	____
7. Do you do well at math and detail?	____	____
8. Do you get depressed easily?	____	____

If your answer to question 1 is yes and you answered yes to questions 2-4, your primary temperament is probably sanguine. If you answered yes to question 1 but had only one yes in questions 2-4, you are probably a choleric temperament.

If you answered no to question 1 and yes to questions 6-8, your primary temperament is probably melancholy. But if you said yes to 5 and you do not get depressed very often, your predominant temperament is likely phlegmatic.

CHAPTER 4

Determining Your Strengths and Weaknesses

Dr. Henry Brandt, a Christian psychologist, has probably helped more people than any other person in that profession. He certainly had a significant influence on this writer's life, both personally and in my role as a family counselor. He made a profound statement about maturity that I have never forgotten. He defines a mature person in relation to his attitude toward his own strengths and weaknesses: *"A mature person is one who is sufficiently objective about himself to know both his strengths and his weaknesses and has created a planned program for overcoming his weaknesses."*

We will now examine both your potential weaknesses and your potential strengths. Knowing both your strengths and weaknesses is the first giant step toward becoming that mature person you have always wanted to be.

The chart we studied earlier listed ten strengths and ten weaknesses for each temperament. There are more, but based on my counseling, testing of thousands of people, and many years of observation, I have selected these as the most common. First let's examine the strengths of each temperament.

SPARKY SANGUINE'S STRENGTHS

Sparky is not just an extrovert, he is a super-extrovert. Everything he does is superficial and external. He laughs loudly and dominates every conversation whether he has anything meaningful to say or not. He loves the limelight and excels at public speaking. He rarely waits for others to speak first, but usually is the first to initiate a conversation.

Mr. Sanguine's ability to respond to others is instantaneous. If he catches another person looking at him, he always responds with a nod, wink, or greeting. No one enjoys life more than Sparky Sanguine. He never seems to lose his childlike curiosity for the things that surround him. Even the unpleasant things of life can be forgotten by his change of environment. It is a rare occasion when he does not awaken in a lively mood, and he will often be found whistling or singing his way through life.

The natural trait of Mr. Sanguine that produces both his hearty and optimistic disposition is defined by Dr. Hallesby, a European authority on this subject: "The sanguine person has a God-given ability to live in the present." He easily forgets the past, and is seldom frustrated or fearful of future difficulties. The sanguine person is optimistic.

He is easily inspired to engage in new plans and projects, and his boundless enthusiasm often carries others along with him. If yesterday's project has failed, he is confident that the project he is working on today will definitely succeed. The outgoing, handshaking, backslapping customs of the cheerful sanguine stem basically from his genuine love for people. He enjoys being around others, sharing in their joys and sorrows, and he likes to make new friends. No one makes a better first impression.

One of the greatest assets of Mr. Sanguine is that he has a tender, compassionate heart. No one responds more genuinely to the needs of others than the sanguine. He is able to share the emotional experiences, both good and bad, of others.

The sincerity of Mr. Sanguine is often misunderstood by others. They are deceived by his sudden changes of emotion, and they fail to understand that he is genuinely responding to the emotions of others. No one can love you more nor forget you faster than a sanguine. The world is enriched by these cheerful, responsive people. When motivated and disciplined by God, they can be great servants of Jesus Christ.

ROCKY CHOLERIC'S STRENGTHS
Mr. Choleric is usually a self-disciplined individual with a strong tendency toward self-determination. He is very confident in his own ability and very aggressive.

Once having embarked upon a project, he has a tenacious ability that keeps him doggedly driving in one direction. His singleness of purpose often results in accomplishment.

The choleric temperament is given over almost exclusively to the practical aspects of life. Everything to him is considered in the light of its utilitarian purpose, and he is happiest when engaged in some worthwhile project. He has a keen mind for organization but finds detail work distressing. Many of his decisions are reached by intuition more than by analytical reasoning.

Mr. Choleric has strong leadership tendencies. His forceful will tends to dominate a group, he is a good judge of people, and he is quick and bold in emergencies. He not only will readily accept leadership when it is placed on him, but will often be the first to volunteer for it. If he does not become too arrogant or bossy, others respond well to his practical direction.

When Rocky sets his mind to do something, he never gives up; just about the time his optimism has come home to engulf him in impossibility, he doggedly burrows out another way. And if people don't agree with him, that's just too bad—he is going to do it with or without them. What other people think of him or his projects makes very little difference to him.

No one is more practical than a choleric. He seems to have a utilitarian mentality. He has strong workaholic tendencies. Mr. Choleric's outlook on life, based on his natural feeling of self-confidence, is almost always one of optimism. He has such an adventuresome spirit that he thinks nothing of leaving a secure position for the challenge of the unknown. Adversity does not discourage him. Instead, it whets his appetite and makes him even more determined to achieve his objective.

MARTIN MELANCHOLY'S STRENGTHS

Usually a melancholy has the highest IQ of any member in his family. He may be musical, artistic, or athletic. Sometimes you will find all these traits in one individual.

Mr. Melancholy has by far the richest and most sensitive nature of all the temperaments. A higher percentage of geniuses are melancholy than any other type. He particularly excels in the fine arts, with a vast appreciation for life's cultural values. He is emotionally responsive, but unlike the sanguine is motivated to reflective thinking through his emotions. Mr. Melancholy is particularly adept at creative thinking, and during high emotional peaks will often launch into an invention or creative production that is worthwhile and wholesome.

Mr. Melancholy has strong perfectionist tendencies. His standard of excellence exceeds others', and his requirements of acceptability in any field are often higher than either he or anyone else can maintain. The analytical abilities of the melancholy, combined with his perfectionist tendencies, make him a "hound for detail." Whenever a project is suggested, Mr. Melancholy can analyze it in a few moments and pick out every potential problem.

A melancholy person can always be depended upon to finish his job in the prescribed time or to carry his end of the load. Mr. Melancholy rarely seeks the limelight, but prefers to do the behind-the-scenes task. He often chooses a very sacrificial vocation for life, for he has an unusual desire to give himself to the betterment of his fellowmen.

He is prone to be reserved and seldom volunteers his opinion or ideas. Melancholy temperaments are extremely self-disciplined individuals. They rarely eat too much or indulge their own comforts. When they engage in a task, they will work around the clock to meet deadlines and their high, self-imposed standards. One of the reasons they can go into a deep depression after completion of a big project is because they have so neglected themselves seeing the task to completion by going without sleep, food, and diversion that they are literally exhausted physically and emotionally.

PHIL PHLEGMATIC'S STRENGTHS
Just because they are superintroverts does not mean phlegmatics are not strong. Actually the phlegmatic's calm and unexcited nature is a vital asset. There are things he can do and vocations he can pursue that extroverts could never do. Phlegmatics rarely, if

ever, leap before they look. They are thinkers and planners.

Phil is a born diplomat. Conciliatory by nature, he does not like confrontation and would rather negotiate than fight. He has a knack for defusing the hostile and excitable types and is a walking example that "a soft answer turns away wrath."

The unexcited good humor of the phlegmatic keeps him from being intensely involved with life so that he can often see humor in the most mundane experiences. He seems to have a superb inborn sense of timing in the art of humor and a stimulating imagination.

Mr. Phlegmatic is dependability itself. Not only can he be depended upon to always be his cheerful, good-natured self, but he can be depended upon to fulfill his obligations and time schedules. Like the melancholy, he is a very faithful friend, and although he does not get too involved with others he rarely proves disloyal.

Mr. Phlegmatic is also practical and efficient. Not prone to making sudden decisions, he has a tendency to find the practical way to accomplish an objective with the least amount of effort. He often does his best work under circumstances that would cause other types to "crack." His work always bears the hallmark of neatness and efficiency. Although he is not a perfectionist, he does have exceptionally high standards of accuracy and precision.

The administrative or leadership capabilities of a phlegmatic are seldom discovered because he is not assertive and doesn't push himself. But once given the responsibility, he has a real ability to get people to work together productively and in an organized manner.

THE REVERSE SIDE OF STRENGTHS

The variety of strengths provided by the four temperament types keeps the world functioning properly. No one personality type is more desirable than another. Each one has its vital strengths and makes its worthwhile contribution to life.

Someone facetiously pointed out this sequence of events involving the four temperaments: "The hard-driving choleric produces the inventions of the genius-prone melancholy, which are sold by the personable sanguine and enjoyed by the easygoing phlegmatic."

The strengths of the four temperaments make each of them attractive, and we can be grateful that we all possess some of these strengths. But there is more to the story! As important as are the temperament strengths, even more important, for our purposes, are their weaknesses. It is our intent to contrast the strengths of these personality categories with their weaknesses. Our purpose in so doing is to help you diagnose your own weaknesses and develop a planned program for overcoming them.

This will doubtless be the most painful section in this book, for no one likes to be confronted with his weaknesses. But if we think of ourselves only in terms of the strengths of our temperaments, we will develop a faulty view of ourselves. Everyone has weaknesses.

SPARKY SANGUINE'S WEAKNESSES

Sanguines are voted "most likely to succeed" in high school, but often fail in life. Their tendency to be weak-willed and undisciplined will finally destroy them unless it is overcome. Since they are highly emotional, exude considerable natural charm, and are prone to be what one psychologist called "touchers" (they tend to touch people as they talk to them), they commonly have a great appeal for the opposite sex and consequently face sexual temptation more than others. Weakness of will and lack of discipline make it easier for them to be deceitful, dishonest, and undependable.

They tend to overeat and gain weight, finding it most difficult to remain on a diet. Someone has said, "Without self-discipline, there is no such thing as success." Lack of discipline is Mr. Sanguine's greatest weakness.

The only temperament more emotional than a sanguine is a melancholy, but he isn't anywhere near as expressive as Sparky Sanguine. Not only can Sparky cry at the drop of a hat (one pro football player's wife won't watch a sad film on TV with her husband, because "his blubbering embarrasses me!"), but his spark of anger can instantly become a raging inferno. A lack of emotional consistency usually limits him vocationally.

Every human being is plagued with egotism, but sanguines have a double dose of the problem. That's why a God-centered Sparky is easily detected; he will reflect an unnatural spirit of humility that is refreshing.

Sanguines are notoriously disorganized and always on the move. They seldom plan ahead but usually take things as they come. They rarely profit by past mistakes and seldom look ahead. As one man said, "They are a disorganized accident waiting to happen."

Wherever Sparky works or lives, things are in a disastrous state of disarray. He can never find his tools, even though they are right where he left them. Sparky's garage, bedroom, closet, and office are disaster areas unless he has an efficient wife and secretary to pick up after him. His egotism usually makes him a sharp dresser, but if his friends or customers could see the room where he dressed, they would fear that someone had been killed in the explosion.

How does Sparky Sanguine get by with that kind of living? The way he handles all confrontations caused by his temperament—a disarming smile, a pat on the back, a funny story, and a restless move to the next thing that sparks his interest. The sanguine will never become a perfectionist, but God can help bring more planning and order into his life. And when that happens, Sparky is a much happier person—not only with others but also with himself.

Behind that superextroverted personality that frequently overpowers other people, giving him a false reputation as a very self-confident person, Sparky Sanguine is really quite insecure. His insecurity is often the source of his vile profanity.

Sanguines are not usually fearful of personal injury and often resort to outlandish feats of daring and heroism. Their fears most often arise in the area of personal failure, rejection, or disapproval. That's why they often follow an obnoxious display of conversation with an equally mindless statement. Rather than face your disapproval, they are hoping to cover up the first goof with something that will gain your approval.

Perhaps the sanguine's most treacherous trait, one that really stifles his spiritual potential, is his weak or flexible conscience. He usually is able to talk others into his way of thinking, earning him the reputation of being the world's greatest con artist. When things go wrong, he has no difficulty convincing himself that whatever he did was justified. He "bends the truth" until any similarity between his story and the facts is totally coincidental; yet this rarely bothers him, for he cons himself into believing that "the end justifies the means."

Others often find it incredible that he can lie, cheat, or steal, yet seldom endure a sleepless night. That is why he frequently walks over the rights of others and rarely hesitates to take advantage of other people.

Sooner or later, Sparky Sanguine will weave a web of deceit that will produce his own destruction. The Bible says, "Be not deceived; God is not mocked; for whatsoever a man soweth, that shall he also reap" (Gal. 6:7). The only way to conquer that problem is to concentrate on truth and honesty. Every time a man lies or cheats, it becomes easier—and the next temptation is bigger.

Sparky Sanguine's penchant for exaggeration, embellishment, and plain old-fashioned deceit catches up with him most quickly in his marriage and family. While he may fool those who see him occasionally, it is impossible for him to cheat and deceive his way through life without teaching his wife and children that they cannot depend on his word.

One of the nine necessary building blocks in any love relationship (according to 1 Corinthians 13:4-8) is trust. Part of the reason the Bible speaks so frequently on the subject of truth or honesty is that it not only produces the necessary clear conscience all people need, but it creates the kind of foundation on which lasting and enjoyable interpersonal relationships are made.

ROCKY CHOLERIC'S WEAKNESSES

Cholerics can be extremely hostile people. Some learn to control their anger, but eruption into violence is always a possibility with them. If their strong will is not brought into control by proper parental discipline as children, they develop angry, tumultuous habits that plague them all through life. It doesn't take them long to learn that others are usually afraid of their angry outbursts and thus they may use wrath as a weapon to get what they want—which is usually their own way. The choleric can cause pain to others and enjoy it. His wife is usually afraid of him, and he tends to terrify his children.

Rocky Choleric often reminds me of a walking Mount Vesuvius, constantly gurgling until, provoked, he spills out his bitter lava all over someone or something. He is a door slammer, a table pounder, a horn blower. Any person or thing that gets in his way, retards his progress, or fails to perform up to the level of his expectations will feel the eruption of his wrath.

No one utters more caustic comments than a sarcastic choleric! He is usually ready with a cutting comment that can wither the insecure and devastate the less combative. Even Sparky Sanguine is no match for him, because Sparky isn't cruel or mean. Rocky will rarely hesitate to tell a person off or chop him to bits. Consequently, he leaves a path of damaged psyches and fractured egos wherever he goes.

It is a happy choleric (and his family members) who discovers that the tongue is either a vicious weapon or a tool of healing. Once he learns the importance of his verbal approval and encouragement to others, he will seek to control his speech—until he gets angry, whereupon he discovers with the Apostle James that "the tongue can no man tame; it is an unruly evil, full of deadly poison" (James 3:8). Ready speech and an angry spirit often combine to make a choleric very profane.

The milk of human kindness has all but dried up in the veins of a choleric. He is the most unaffectionate of all the temperaments and becomes emotionally spastic at the thought of any public show of emotion. Marital affection to him means a kiss at the wedding and on every fifth anniversary thereafter. His emotional rigidity rarely permits him the expression of tears. He usually stops crying at the age of eleven or twelve and finds it difficult to understand others when they are moved to tears.

Similar to his natural lack of love is the choleric's tendency to be insensitive to others' needs and inconsiderate of their feelings. When a choleric is sensitive and considerate, he can be a great blessing to others, for, as we have seen, what he thinks of others is of vital importance to them. By nature Rocky Choleric has the hide of a rhinoceros. However, God can help him become kind and tenderhearted.

The choleric's natural determination is a temperament asset that stands him in good stead throughout life, but it can make him opinionated and bullheaded. Since he has an intuitive sense, he usually makes up his mind quickly (without adequate analysis and deliberation), and once made up, it is almost impossible to change. No type more typifies the old cliche: "Don't confuse me with the facts; my mind is made up."

One of the undesirable characteristics of the choleric involves his inclination to be crafty if necessary to get his own way. He rarely takes no for an answer and will often resort to any means necessary to achieve his ends. If he has to juggle his figures and bend the truth, he rarely hesitates, for to him the end justifies the means.

Since he easily comes to conclusions, he finds great delight in making decisions for other people and forcing them to conform to his will. If you work for a choleric, you rarely wonder what he wants you to do, for he tells you five times before eight-thirty in the morning—and usually at the top of his lungs.

The Rocky Cholerics of life are very effective people if their weaknesses are not indulged until they become a dominating lifestyle. When they are influenced by God, their tendencies toward willfulness and harshness are replaced by a gentleness which verifies clearly that they are controlled by something other than their own natural temperament.

MARTIN MELANCHOLY'S WEAKNESSES

The admirable qualities of perfectionism and conscientiousness often carry with them the serious disadvantages of negativism, pessimism, and a spirit of criticism. Anyone who has worked with a gifted melancholy can anticipate that his first reaction to anything will be negative or pessimistic. This one trait limits a melancholy's vocational performance more than any other. The minute a new idea or project is presented, his analytical ability ignites and he begins to concoct every problem and difficulty that may be encountered in the effort.

The most damaging influence upon a person's mind, in my opinion, is criticism; and melancholies have to fight that spirit constantly. I have observed that the most psychologically disturbed children come from homes of predominantly melancholy or choleric parents. Cholerics are hard to please; melancholies are impossible to satisfy. Even when the children bring home B's and B plusses, the parents will grimace with dissatisfaction because they didn't get A's. Instead of commending their wives and encouraging them, melancholies criticize, carp, and censure. Even when they realize the importance of their approval to both wife and children, it is hard for them to offer it because they cannot endure the hypocritical taint of saying something that isn't 100 percent true.

The same high standard is usually turned inward by a melancholy, making him very dissatisfied with himself. Self-examination, of course, is a healthy thing. But the melancholy is not satisfied to examine himself; he dissects himself with a continuing barrage of introspection until he has no self-confidence or self-esteem left. Everything in life is interpreted by the melancholy in relation to himself. He tends to compare himself with others on looks, talent, and intellect, invariably feeling deficient because it never occurs to him that he compares himself to the best of another's traits and fails to evaluate their weaknesses.

His self-centered trait, together with his sensitive nature, makes a melancholy thin-skinned and touchy at times. Although not as expressive of his anger as the sanguine or choleric, he is very capable of long-term seething and slow-burning anger in the form of revengeful thinking patterns and self-persecution reveries. If indulged long enough, this can make him manic-depressive or at least erupt into an angry outburst that is unlike his normally gentle nature.

One of the most prominent characteristics of a melancholy concerns his mood swings. On some occasions he is so "high" that he acts like a sanguine; on others he is so "down" that he feels like sliding under the door rather than opening it. The older he gets (unless transformed by a vital relationship to Jesus Christ), the more he is prone to experience dark moods. During such times he is gloomy, irritable, unhappy, and all but impossible to please. Such moods make him particularly vulnerable to depression.

Anyone with a depression problem, particularly a melancholy, should make 1 Thessalonians 5:18 a way of life: "In everything give thanks: for this is the will of God in Christ

Jesus concerning you." You cannot rejoice and give thanks over something while maintaining a state of depression.

No other temperament is so apt to be rigid, implacable, and uncompromising to the point of unreasonableness as the melancholy. He is intolerant and impatient with those who do not see things his way; consequently he finds it difficult to be a team player and is often a loner in the business world, but at home it is a different matter. A wife and children subjected to such rigid standards will often become insecure and unhappy and sometimes give up on him. Once he learns that flexibility and cooperation are the oil that makes interpersonal relationships run smoothly, he is a much happier person and so are those around him.

We have already seen that the melancholy is an idealist, a trait we list as a strength. However, on the other side of that characteristic, he is apt to be impractical and theoretical, often campaigning for an ideal that is so altruistic it will never work. A melancholy should always subject his plans to the practicality test.

PHIL PHLEGMATIC'S WEAKNESSES
The most obvious of Phil Phlegmatic's weaknesses and that which caused Hippocrates (who originated the idea of the four temperaments) to label him *phlegm* (slow or sluggish) is his apparent lack of drive and ambition. Although he always seems to do what is ex-

pected of him, he will rarely do more. Rarely does he instigate an activity, but thinks up excuses to avoid getting involved with the activities of others.

More than any other type, the phlegmatic is vulnerable to the law of inertia: "A body at rest tends to stay at rest." He needs to reverse that trend with premeditated activity. Both he and his family will benefit by such efforts.

No one likes to be hurt, and that is particularly true of Phil Phlegmatic. Although not as sensitive as a melancholy, he does have a thin skin and accordingly learns early in life to live like a turtle—that is, to build a hard shell of self-protection to shield him from all outside griefs or affronts. But even a turtle could give Phil a valuable piece of advice: "You can never go anywhere unless you stick your neck out." Nor will you ever help anyone else unless you risk the possibility of an emotional injury.

One of the less obvious weaknesses of the phlegmatic is his selfishness. Every temperament faces the problem of selfishness, but Phil is particularly afflicted with the disease, though he is so gracious and proper that few people who don't live with him are aware of it. Selfishness makes him self-indulgent and unconcerned about his family's need for activity.

No one can be more stubborn than a phlegmatic, but he is so diplomatic about it that he may proceed halfway through life before others catch on. He almost never openly confronts another person or refuses to do something but he will somehow manage to sidestep the demand. In church administration I have found this gracious, kindly, placid individual to be most exasperating at times. He will smile as I detail the program, even nod his head as if he understands, and then walk away and ignore the mandate. He simply will do it his way—quite affably and with less contention than any other type, but definitely his way. In a family situation, phlegmatics never yell or argue; they just drag their feet or set their legs and will not budge.

Beneath the gracious surface of a diplomatic phlegmatic beats a very fearful heart. This fear tendency often keeps him from venturing out on his own to make full use of his potential.

Now you have the bad news: all personality types have weaknesses—at least ten, according to their temperament. But there is a power that can enable you to improve and to emphasize your strengths. Read on!

STRENGTHENING YOUR WEAKNESSES
One thing about temperament—it never changes. If your parents' genes combined to make you a ChlorSan, a MelPhleg, or a San-MelPhleg, you will never be anything else. Like your appearance, height, and IQ, your personality type will be a part of you as long as you live. And remember, your temperament probably has more to do with your cur-

rent behavior than anything else in your life. The rest is the result of your childhood training, home life, education, motivation, and other influences. The following formula will put it all together for you.

BEHAVIOR FORMULA

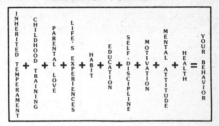

INHERITED TEMPERAMENT + CHILDHOOD TRAINING + PARENTAL LOVE + LIFE'S EXPERIENCES + HABIT + EDUCATION + SELF-DISCIPLINE + MOTIVATION + MENTAL ATTITUDE + HEALTH = YOUR BEHAVIOR

As you look over this list, you are probably struck with the realization that you have very little control over most of the ingredients in this formula. Don't be deceived! It is true that you cannot change your temperament, but there are three things in that formula that you do control and so can improve yourself and change your life: motivation, mental attitude, and habit. Let's look more closely at the first of these.

LIVE UP TO YOUR POTENTIAL
When God created Adam, he made him unique among all other living creatures. He gave him a soul. This soul not only has a capacity for God but is a source of external motivation that is all but untapped by most people today. But it does account for the tremendous transformation that occurs in

people when they have a "born again" experience with Jesus Christ. To understand this, you must visualize the four parts of human nature as described in the Bible.

Jesus Christ knew more about human nature than anyone who has ever lived. He said, "Thou shalt love the Lord thy God with all thy heart, and with all thy soul, and with all thy mind, and with all thy strength" (Mark 12:30). Compare carefully the four aspects of human nature: heart, soul, mind, strength. Notice these on the following chart.

THE NATURAL MAN

1) Heart: The emotional center—source of feeling and motivation. "As a man thinks in his heart so is he."

2) Soul: Source of human life and the will. God has given each person sovereignty over his own will. Your self is by nature the control mechanism of your will.

4) Strength: This refers to the perishable part of man, or that which we see the most.

3) Mind: The most incredible organ in the body. It contains twelve billion brain cells, and how you fill those cells influences your feelings, which in turn influence everything you do.

Your inherited temperament probably resides in the heart, where it influences the method of your thinking—not the content. It can be influenced by the mind, soul, and heart. It is what the Bible means when it speaks of "the flesh" or "nature" or "natural man."

Guilt
Fear
Emptiness
Misery
Purposelessness
Confusion

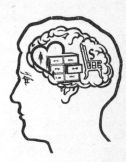

THE NATURAL MAN

Christ is not in the natural man; he is outside his life. Without Christ, a person will experience the guilt, fear, emptiness, misery, purposelessness, confusion, and other negative feelings pictured above. The amount of negative feelings will depend on his willfulness and sin. His greatest need is his emptiness—his unfilled "God-shaped vacuum" that Pascal said was in the heart of every man and can be filled with no one save Jesus Christ. The emptiness that plagues mankind all through life not only cheats a person out of God's daily presence in his life, but God's power to improve his temperament.

71

God never forces his way into a person's life; he leaves it to an individual to decide whether or not to receive Christ as his Savior and Lord. But if you believe Jesus Christ died for your sins and rose again the third day, you can humbly repent of your sins and submit your will to him by praying a simple but beautiful prayer like this: *"O God, I know I am a sinner and have willfully disobeyed you many times. I believe Jesus died for my sins and rose again that I might have eternal life. Therefore, I invite you to come into my life to both save me from my sins and to direct my future. Today I give myself to you."*

"As many as received him [Jesus], to them gave he the power to become the sons of God" (John 1:12). All who believe in him are born again and have two natures. The new one is the new man in Christ, opening up a whole new source of power. The old nature still wants to sin.

Both natures are alive. Which one is dominant depends on which one you feed the most. If you feed the old nature, don't be surprised when the weaknesses of your personality type dominate you. If, however, you feed your new nature the spiritual food of the Bible and things pertaining to God, your new nature will become so dominant it will overcome your natural weaknesses, enabling God to make maximum use of your inherited strengths.

Making Your Personality Work for You

ON THE JOB

Next to lack of employment, the worst thing that can happen to a person is to have the wrong job. It is incredible how many people despise their work. No wonder it becomes such drudgery to them.

One of the ways to avoid vocational frustration, or feeling like a round peg in a square hole, is to know your personality type and its natural vocational possibilities. Then find work or a profession that allows you to express your natural characteristics.

WHERE DO YOU BELONG?

The following rule of thumb will give you general guidance:

- SANGUINES: People-oriented salesman types who excel in public relations, people-helping, or anything that requires charisma.
- CHOLERICS: Strong natural leaders who are goal- or project-oriented individuals and like to manage people.

73

- MELANCHOLIES: Creative, analytical individuals with strong perfectionist tendencies who often have aesthetic traits.
- PHLEGMATICS: Cool, detail-oriented individuals who tend to limit themselves. They can do statistical, microscopic work that would drive others berserk.

SPARKY SANGUINE'S VOCATIONAL POTENTIAL

The world is enriched by sanguines with their cheeriness and natural charisma. They usually make excellent salesmen, and more than any other personality type seem attracted to that profession. If you ever want to watch Mr. Sanguine in action on the job, just visit your local used-car dealer. Two-thirds of his salesmen are probably sanguines.

In addition to being good salesmen, sanguines make excellent actors, entertainers, and ministers. They are outstanding masters of ceremonies, auctioneers, and sometimes leaders (if properly blended with another temperament). They are increasingly in demand within the political arena, where natural charisma has proven advantageous on television and radio. Sanguines also excel in the people-helping professions; for example, they are very good as hospital workers.

Key to effectiveness. Sanguines are not detail-oriented. The sales manager who wants his sanguine employee to "fill in the blanks" on the business form is often frustrated. Sanguines would much rather be out on the golf course with a client than strategizing, analyzing, or filling out forms.

While it's true most sanguines are not *natural* detail hounds, they can do better. It is all a matter of self-discipline. The sanguine has the tendency to indulge his weaknesses and refuse to discipline himself. The sanguine often limits his ultimate potential in this way.

The key to effectiveness for the sanguine is that extra effort at self-discipline.

ROCKY CHOLERIC'S VOCATIONAL POTENTIAL

Any profession that requires leadership, motivation, and productivity is open to a choleric, provided it does not demand too much attention to detail or analytical planning. Committee meetings and long-range planning bore him, for he is a doer. Although not usually a craftsman (which requires a degree of perfection and efficiency usually beyond his capability), he often serves as a supervisor for craftsmen. He usually enjoys construction because he is so productive and will frequently end up as a foreman or project supervisor.

Most entrepreneurs are cholerics. They formulate the ideas and are venturesome enough to launch out in new directions. They don't limit themselves to their own ideas either, but sometimes overhear a creative idea from someone who is not sufficiently adventurous to initiate a new business or project.

Once a choleric learns to delegate responsibility to others and discovers that he is able to accomplish more through other people, he can complete an amazing amount of work. He would rather get a number of things finished 70 to 80 percent than complete just a few things 100 percent.

Key to effectiveness. Rocky Choleric is a natural motivator of other people. He oozes self-confidence, is extremely goal-conscious, and can inspire others to envision his goals. His primary weakness as a leader is that he is hard to please and tends to run roughshod over other people. If he only knew how others look to him for approval and encouragement, he would spend more time acknowledging their accomplishments, which would generate even greater dedication from his colleagues.

Unfortunately the choleric tends to think

that approval and encouragement will lead to complacency. He tends to resort to excessive criticism as a corrective. He must learn that criticism is usually a demotivator. The key to Rocky Choleric's effectiveness on the job is his discovery that people require reassurance and stimulation in order to perform at the height of their potential. If he discovers this simple fact, his leadership will radically improve.

MARTIN MELANCHOLY'S VOCATIONAL POTENTIAL

As a general rule, no other temperament has a higher IQ, creativity, or imagination than a melancholy, and no one else is as capable of perfectionism. Most of the world's great composers, artists, musicians, inventors, actors, philosophers, theoreticians, theologians, scientists, and dedicated educators have been predominantly melancholies.

Any vocation that requires perfection, self-sacrifice, and creativity is open to a Martin Melancholy. Almost any humanitarian vocation will attract melancholies to its staff. For years I have watched doctors, and although there are bound to be exceptions, almost every doctor I know is either predominantly or at least secondarily a melancholy.

Not all melancholies, of course, enter the professions or arts. Many become craftsmen of high quality—finish carpenters, bricklayers, plumbers, plasterers, nurserymen, mechanics, and engineers.

In the building trades, the melancholy may want to supervise construction. However, he would be better off hiring a project supervisor who works better with people and then spend his own time on the drawing board.

Key to effectiveness. The melancholy tends to place self-imposed restrictions upon his potential by underestimating himself and exaggerating his obstacles.

Martin Melancholy becomes frustrated by the usual personnel problems and, with his unrealistic perfectionist demands, adds to them.

His key to effectiveness is accepting the unique contributions of other people, although they may not measure up to his perfectionistic standards. In addition, he should give himself to the kind of positive thinking that puts problems and obstacles in proper, and manageable, perspective.

PHIL PHLEGMATIC'S VOCATIONAL POTENTIAL

The world has benefited greatly from the gracious nature of Phil Phlegmatic. In his quiet way he has proved to be a fulfiller of the dreams of others. He is a master at anything that requires meticulous patience and daily routine.

Most elementary school teachers are phlegmatics. Who but a phlegmatic could have the patience necessary to teach a group of first-graders to read? The gentle nature of the phlegmatic ensures the ideal atmosphere for such learning. This is not only true in the elementary level, but in both high school and college, particularly in math, physics, grammar, literature, language classes, and other areas of teaching and study. It is not uncommon to find phlegmatics as school administrators, librarians, counselors, and college department heads. Phlegmatics seem drawn to the field of education.

Engineering also appeals to phlegmatics. Attracted to planning and calculation, they make good structural engineers, sanitation experts, chemical engineers, draftsmen, mechanical and civil engineers, and statisticians. Most phlegmatics have excellent mechanical aptitude and thus become good mechanics, tool-and-die specialists, craftsmen, carpenters, electricians, plasterers, glassblowers, watch and camera repair specialists.

In recent years, management has begun to learn that phlegmatics in their employ often make excellent foremen, supervisors, and managers of people. Because they are diplomatic and unabrasive, people work well with them. When given positions of leadership, they seem to bring order out of chaos and produce a working harmony conducive to increased productivity. They are well-organized, never come to a meeting unprepared or late, work well under pressure, and are extremely dependable. Phlegmatics often stay with one company for their entire working career.

Key to effectiveness. An interesting aspect of the phlegmatic's leadership ability is that they rarely volunteer for authority, which is why I call them "reluctant leaders." Secretly, a phlegmatic may aspire for a promotion, but it would be against his nature to push for it. Instead, he may patiently wait until discord and ineptness on another's part make a mess of things; then he may be asked to step in and take control. Unfortunately, for many phlegmatics opportunity never knocks— partly because the phlegmatic has this very reluctance to step foward. The phlegmatic's key to effectiveness is learning to be more assertive and taking responsibility when it is available to him.

MARRIAGE

What could be more opposite than male and female? Yet they still attract each other after thousands of years. In fact, the future of the race is dependent upon such attraction. Unfortunately, many couples fail to realize that their physical differences are only symbolic of the many other differences in their natures, the most significant of which are their temperaments.

A negative is never attracted to another negative, and positives repel each other in any field—electricity, chemistry, and particularly temperament. Instead, negatives are attracted to positives and vice versa. I have found this almost universally true of the temperaments.

For instance, a sanguine would seldom marry another sanguine, for both are such natural extroverts that they would be competing for the same stage in life, and no one would be sitting in the audience. Cholerics, on the other hand, make such severe demands on other people that they not only wouldn't marry each other, they probably would never date—at least not more than once. They would spend all their time arguing about everything and vying for control or authority in their relationship. Two melancholies might marry, but it is very unlikely. Their analytical traits find negative qualities in others, and thus neither would pursue the other. Two phlegmatics would rarely marry, for they would both die of old age before one got up enough steam to propose.

In the Western world, where couples choose their own partners, you will find that generally opposite temperaments attract each other. I surveyed several hundred couples. *Ordinarily I found that sanguines were attracted to melancholies and cholerics to phlegmatics,* although that is by no means universal.

Sanguines, who tend to be disorganized and undisciplined themselves, are apt to admire careful, consistent, and detail-conscious melancholies. The latter, in turn, favor outgoing, uninhibited individuals who compensate for the introvert's rigidity and aloofness. The hard-driving choleric is often attracted to the peaceful, unexcited phlegmatic, who in turn admires Rocky's dynamic drive.

After the honeymoon, the problems from this kind of selection begin to surface. Sparky Sanguine is not just warm, friendly, and uninhibited, but forgetful, disorganized, and very undependable. Besides, he gets quite irate if his lady love, a melancholy, asks him to pick up his clothes, put away his tools, or come home on time. Somehow Rocky Choleric's before-marriage "dynamic personality" turns into anger, cruelty, sarcasm, and bullheadedness after marriage. Martin Melancholy's gentleness and well-structured lifestyle become nitpicky and impossible to please after marriage. Philip Phlegmatic's cool, calm, and peaceful ways often seem lazy, unmotivated, and stubborn afterward.

Learning to adapt to your partner's weaknesses while strengthening your own is known as "adjustment in marriage." Hopefully, it will comfort you to know that no matter whom you marry or what temperament you select, you will have to endure this adjustment process to some degree.

STEPS TO A HAPPY MARRIAGE

God is the author of marriage. He intended that it be the happiest, most fulfilling experience in a person's life. And millions have found it so long before anyone discovered temperament. Now that we have this theory to assist us, a happy marriage should be every couple's goal. These steps to personality adjustment will help.

1. Slam the divorce door. Easy divorce has done nothing to help the longevity of marriage. In the state of California I warned our leaders that if they reduced the waiting period for a divorce decree from one year to six months it would double the divorce rate in ten years. I was wrong; we doubled it in seven years.

I have found that as long as the divorce door remains open, it retards the adjustment to a happy marriage. By slamming the door in your mind, you open yourself fully to the resources of God to bring the sparkle of love back into your relationship.

2. Admit to yourself that you are not per-

fect. Humility is the best possible base for establishing any relationship between two people. That is true particularly of marriage, because the couple spends so much time together. True love for another person is built on humility.

A healthy look at your own personality type will enable you to recognize that you have not brought only strengths into your marriage. In fact, you probably have a long way to go toward improving your weaknesses. Realistically facing the fact will help you do step three.

3. Accept the fact that your partner has weaknesses. Repeatedly we have discerned through the study of temperament and personality types that all human beings reflect both strengths and weaknesses. The sooner you face the fact that anyone you marry will have weaknesses to which you must adjust, the sooner you can get to the business of adjusting to your partner. Resist all mental fantasies of, "If only I had married ——— !" or "If only I had married another type of person." That is not a live option, so why not accept your partner's weaknesses?

4. Pray for the strengthening of your partner's weaknesses. God is in the temperament-modification business. If your spouse is a Christian, God is able to provide the strengths he or she needs. But it will never happen if you are on his or her back all the time. If a weakness produces a consistent pattern of behavior such a tardiness, messiness, legalism, negativism, and so on, it may be advisable to talk lovingly to your partner about it once; but after that, just commit the matter to God.

The Bible says, "The effectual fervent prayer of a righteous man availeth much" (James 5:16). As you pray, God will work on your partner.

5. *Apologize when you are wrong.* Everyone makes mistakes! Fortunately, you don't have to be perfect to be a good person or partner. A mature person is one who knows both his strengths and weaknesses and develops a planned program for overcoming his weaknesses. That presumes you will make mistakes. We must ask, then, Are you mature enough to take full responsibility for what you have done? If in anger you have offended your partner in word or in deed, you need to apologize. An apology reaches into another's heart and mind to remove the root of bitterness that otherwise would fester and grow until it choked your relationship. That is why the Bible exhorts, "Confess your faults one to another . . ." (James 5:16).

6. *Verbalize your love.* Everyone needs love and will profit from hearing it verbalized frequently. This is particularly true of women, whatever their personality type.

I once counseled a brilliant engineer, a father of five, whose wife left him for another man whose salary was one-third her husband's. After a bit of probing, I learned that he had not expressed his love for ten years. Why? He didn't think it was necessary. Verbalizing love is not only a necessity for holding a couple together, but an enrichment of their relationship.

After five or ten years of marriage the man is responsible for 80 percent or more of his wife's self-acceptance. That is more important than most people realize, for if a person doesn't love and accept himself he will have a very difficult time loving and accepting others. And the best way for a man to help his wife gain self-acceptance is by verbally reassuring her of his acceptance and love. Instead of harping on her weaknesses and beating her down continually, he should comment positively on her strengths. It enriches her self-esteem and motivates her to try harder.

Some ill-advised men are afraid of the procedure, thinking it will make her complacent. Just the opposite is true. Women thrive on approval, compliments, and love. Disapproval and humiliation destroy; approval enriches. The man who wants a wife who thinks well of herself can help her become that way.

Adjusting to another person, particularly someone of a type opposite to your own, is not easy and it is not done quickly. But like anything of real value, it is worth the investment. And someday you will realize you are married to your best friend. That is the ideal marriage.

UNDER PRESSURE
Pressure is a part of life; no one escapes it. We are more conscious of it in this day of jet

travel, computers, and frenetic activity than those who lived in farming communities fifty years ago. No matter where you live or what you do in life, you will experience pressure; it is inescapable.

But all temperaments do not face pressure the same way.

SPARKY
SANGUINE
FACING
PRESSURE

Sanguines rarely get ulcers; we've already seen that they usually give them to everyone else. Since people are a major cause of pressure and sanguines love to be around people, they are never far from pressure, which usually they helped to create.

These lighthearted people are often very disorganized, generally arrive late for meetings, and are rarely prepared for whatever they are supposed to do. Unfortunately, each time they get by with improvising under pressure, they learn that advance planning is not really crucial for success. This could be the reason why sanguines are often "short-termers." That is, they run out of material after a time and must move on to their next job.

Sanguines are quick of speech and often use their vocal chords to defend themselves when pressed. More aggressive types learn that in verbally attacking other people they can often intimidate them into submission; so they cover their mistakes by pressuring others.

One of the most uncomplimentary tendencies of a sanguine under pressure is his difficulty in honestly taking the blame for his mistakes. Because he commands a giant ego, needs the love and admiration of others, and lacks discipline, it is easy for him to pass the buck, blame others for his mistakes, and in some cases lie to get out of a trap. This is why parents of sanguine children need to concentrate on teaching them self-discipline and truth-telling. Otherwise they will develop a flexible conscience.

Some sanguines resort to weepy repentance when confronted with the pressure caused by their unkempt ways. Such repentance is usually short-lived; the sanguine has learned little or nothing from the experience.

Most sanguines cannot endure emotional pressure for very long. They will start talking, tell an unrelated joke, or run away from the problem.

Key to Effectiveness. If sanguines could learn to use pressure as a motivation toward problem-solving, their lives would be greatly enriched. Mistakes do not need to pose a threat to a sanguine; rather, they can guide him to new and better ways of handling situations. Persisting in self-improvement will pay off well in the long-run. I believe sanguines could become 25 to 50 percent more successful in their chosen fields if they would channel their energies into problem-solving rather than problem-dodging.

ROCKY CHOLERIC FACING PRESSURE

No one can create more pressure than a choleric. He thrives on it—until his body breaks down with ulcers, high blood pressure, heart attack, or other physical adversities.

Some of the choleric's high pressure quotient is occasioned by his "god complex." Perhaps it would be better to label it an "omnipotence complex." Cholerics are always overinvolved. They are willing to tackle anything that needs to be done.

Cholerics rarely get depressed when a project fails, because they have other irons in the fire to keep their overly active minds occupied. Instead of wallowing in self-pity over an insult, failure, or rejection, they busy themselves with their next project.

However, this penchant for taking on more than anyone could possibly accomplish often proves to be the cause of greatest pressures. Cholerics are extremely goal-oriented, but unless their secondary temperament is melancholy, they will not be adept at planning, analyzing, and attending to detail. In fact, they usually don't like it. Cholerics are doers. Consequently they may rush into battle before establishing a plan of attack, thus creating a great deal of pressure.

Because they take on excessive loads and fail to delegate responsibility, cholerics tend to take their extra time away from the family. Their ten-hour days soon increase to twelve and fifteen hours, the day off becomes another working day, and vacation time never seems to arrive. The family suffers.

Interpersonal relationships are not a choleric's strength, and work pressures compound this. He tends to be impatient with those less motivated than himself, critical and demanding of others, even unappreciative of people when they do well. If he is an employer, he usually experiences a high turnover at his place of business. His family members tend to give him a wide berth. Cruel and unkind by nature, he can be very cutting and sarcastic under pressure.

Key to Effectiveness. A choleric must establish the best priorities for this life and concentrate on them. A man without priorities may become engrossed in activities that may better have been left alone. The choleric needs to set his priorities in this order:

1. God
2. Spouse
3. Family
4. Vocation

Then he needs to establish clearly defined goals, rejecting creative ideas that do not contribute to the realization of these goals. He also must develop a love for people, learning to encourage others and become interested in them. His time spent on people will be returned to him multiplied, because others will extend themselves in appreciation, thus relieving him of many of his pressures.

MARTIN MELANCHOLY FACING PRESSURE

Like everyone else, melancholies face pressure in life. But because of their sensitive, creative, and perfectionistic ways, everything in life is intensified, especially pressure. Probably no temperament bears more pressure in heart and mind than does the melancholy. This may be why his mortality rate is approximately seven years lower than that of other types.

We have already seen that one's mental

attitude can increase or decrease realistic pressure. That is bad news for a melancholy. One of his biggest problems in life relates to his mental attitude—he is as critical of himself as he is of others.

One of a melancholy's consistent pressures is his desire to do everything perfectly. While commendable to a point, this trait can become maddening to others, for he often spends an inordinate amount of time on trivia or nonessentials at the neglect of more important matters.

The melancholy's penchant for advance planning can drive the rest of the family off a cliff. Everything should be faithfully worried about! He often creates so much pressure contemplating and designing a vacation that all spontaneity and fun are eliminated.

Since a melancholy person is predominantly an introvert, he will rarely externalize his pressures by angrily kicking things, swearing, or screaming—at first. His style is to internalize his pressure, comply with what is immediately expected of him, and mull it over until he gets himself so worked up that he lashes out in a manner totally out of character for him—anything from tears to murder. Some of the most vicious crimes committed by people with no criminal records have been accomplished by melancholies under intense pressure. Fortunately, few melancholies react in violence. Most say things of a cutting, hurtful nature for which they are later very repentant. Others ponder the problem and lapse into sulking silence.

Key to Effectiveness. A melancholy is often so interested in himself and his persistent brand of perfectionism that he has little sympathy for others' mistakes or shortcomings. The key to effectiveness for melancholies under pressure is the acceptance of less-than-perfect circumstances and people—including himself. By tempering their rigid standards, melancholic personalities will be better able to show concern for other people, express their feelings in a positive manner, and free themselves from inner pressure.

PHIL PHLEGMATIC FACING PRESSURE

Phlegmatics detest pressure. In fact, they will do almost anything to avoid it. As we have seen, they do not thrive on controversy, but are peacemakers by nature. Consequently they will always steer around a problem if possible. Unfortunately, ignoring a real problem never makes it disappear.

It is easy to diagnose a sanguine's reaction to pressure, for he explodes loudly enough for everyone to hear and see. Phlegmatics are different; as very "internal" people, they do nothing to excess. For this reason you must observe their responses carefully.

Phlegmatics are apt to blame other people for their mistakes. It's not that they want to be deceitful; they just don't like the pressure of taking the full responsibility for their behavior. The disadvantage of this trait to the phlegmatic himself is that he seldom learns from his behavior. Because blaming others frees him from the immediate pressure, he goes his cheerful way, not admitting that he needs to improve in this regard. As a result, he tends to repeat his mistakes.

Key to Effectiveness. Their compulsion to avoid pressure causes many phlegmatics to become gifted procrastinators. This eventually increases their pressures, because tasks must be completed sooner or later and final decisions have to be made. Some phlegmatics use the old dodge "We need more information" as an excuse for delaying an unpleasant deed. "Remove the pressure, not the problem" often becomes the phlegmatic way of life.

Problems seldom vanish with time. Rather, they tend to become more robust and intimidating than before. I have found that it is usually best to solve such problems when they are still small enough to handle. The key to effectiveness for a phlegmatic is to face pressures squarely as soon as they arise.

OTHER WAYS TO FACE PRESSURE
Whatever your temperament, you will face pressure in life. You cannot change that, nor

are you responsible for it. But you are responsible for the way you respond to pressure regardless of your temperament. For there is one thing more important than your temperament in relation to how you respond to pressure—your mental attitude. And with God's help you can control your mental attitude.

One of the most important truths I have discovered since becoming a Christian is the need to maintain a thankful attitude—about everything. There are only two kinds of people: gripers and thankers. Gripers are never happy; thankers always are.

I am convinced that one cannot be lastingly happy or learn how to control pressure unless he develops the mental habit of thanksgiving. And that's not easy. Personally I have to work at it. After all these years of teaching, writing, and trying to practice a thankful mental attitude, you'd think it would become automatic. Not so!

I look on the development of a habitual mental attitude of thanksgiving as if it were a large boulder which I consciously push uphill every day. If I subconsciously forget thanksgiving, the stone rolls back down the hill a few yards, and I must start pushing again. It gets easier only as I try to be grateful by thanking God for his goodness in the things I understand, and by thanking him by faith for what he is going to do in the things I don't understand.

Thankful living is a matter of daily developing a mental attitude of thanksgiving. It is not only "the will of God" for your life, but the secret to developing a positive mental attitude, which in turn is a vital key to increasing your personality power.

About the Author

DR. TIM LaHAYE is the author of twenty-one books, including *Spirit-Controlled Temperament* and *Transformed Temperaments*. A popular speaker on family life and prophecy, he currently serves as an associate pastor at the Prestonwood Baptist Church of Dallas, Texas, where his Family Enrichment Class is transmitted live via satellite to many churches each Sunday. He is president of the American Coalition for Traditional Values in Washington, D.C.